2nd EDITION
INCREDIBLE ENGLISH

Class Book

1

Sarah Phillips

Kirstie Grainger   **Michaela Morgan**   **Mary Slattery**

OXFORD
UNIVERSITY PRESS

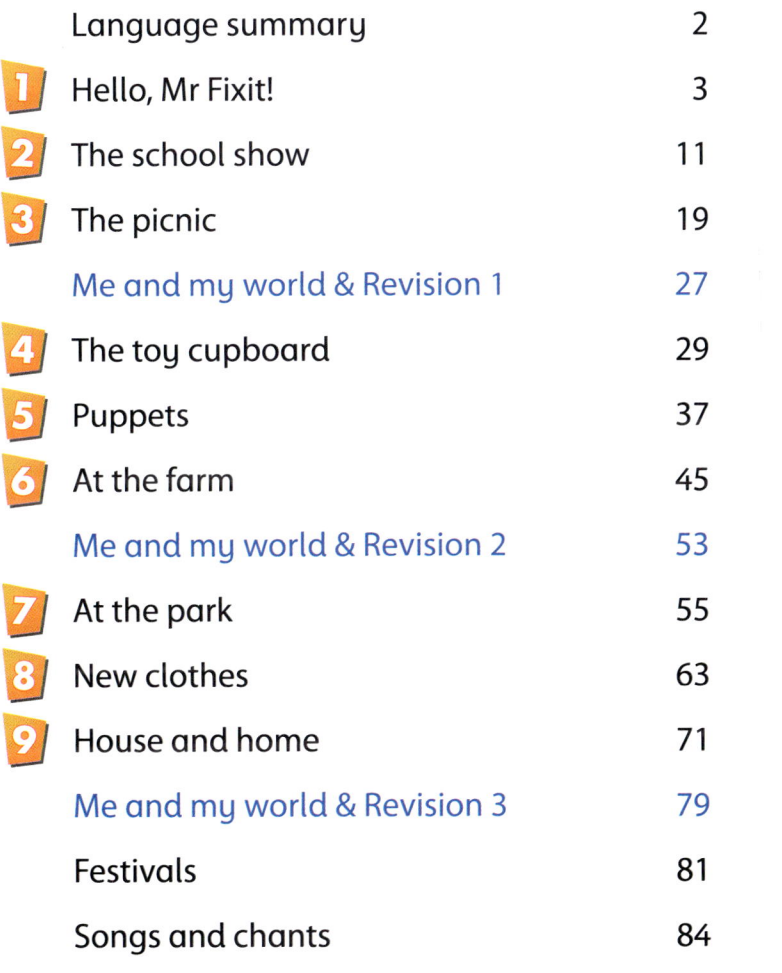

Language summary

1 Hello, Mr Fixit!

Hello. Goodbye. Bye.
What's your name? I'm …
My favourite colour's …
What colour is …? It's …
How many …?

Characters: Fred Flo Titch Poppy Bing Mr Fixit Norton

Colours: red blue green yellow black white orange purple brown pink grey

Numbers: 1 to 12

Shapes: big small triangle square rectangle circle

2 The school show

How old are you? I'm …
Who's this? This is my …
Well done!

Family members: Mum Dad Grandma Grandpa brother sister aunt uncle cousin

People: man woman girl boy

Other: family seat photo picture

3 The picnic

I've got …
Please
Thank you / Thanks
Pass me …
Here you are!
My favourite!

Food and drink: apple banana orange cake juice fizzy drink biscuit sandwich yoghurt chocolate bar sugar cereal bar carrot milk bread roll

Other: lunch picnic naughty swap clean dirty good bad

4 The toy cupboard

Where's my …?
It's here. / It isn't here.
Put the … away!
My turn / Your turn
It's made of …

Toys: car doll ball robot teddy train bike plane computer puppet

Materials: plastic wood metal fabric

Other: share play sing read

5 Puppets

It's got …
Where's the …?
What colour … have you got?

Parts of the body: head body arms legs hands feet fingers toes

Parts of the face: face hair eyes nose mouth ears

Other: move puppet clap stretch touch red (hair) blonde (hair)

6 At the farm

I like …
I don't like …
Let's …

Animals: dog cat hen duck cow sheep goat horse donkey rabbit

Baby animals: foal lamb puppy kitten chick

Other: farm scared of feed brush walk stroke

7 At the park

I can … / I can't …
Can you …? Yes / No
He / She can …
How old is he / she?

Actions: run jump walk hop fly ride a bike kick a ball climb a tree juggle throw a frisbee

Abilities: swim talk draw read write

Other: gate exercise turn around Happy birthday!

8 New clothes

I'm wearing …
What have you got?
What's the weather like?
It's …

Clothes: dress T-shirt shorts trousers jumper skirt shoes socks hat jacket

Weather: hot cold windy raining cloudy

Other: clothes new pair of clown stamp slap tap

9 House and home

Where's …?
He's / She's in the …
What colour is …?
Can I help?

Parts of a house: living room kitchen bathroom bedroom hall garage garden

Places in a town: house bus stop shop school park cinema

Other: washing up tidying up cleaning up

1 Hello, Mr Fixit!

1 **Look and say. Listen and find.** 🔘 1.1
2 **Listen and say.** 🔘 1.2

Norton

WELCOME BACK TO SCHOOL!

Mr Fixit

Titch

Flo

Poppy

Fred

Bing

1 Listen and point. 1.5

I'm Titch!

1 Hello, I'm Flo.
What's your name?
I'm Bing.
I'm Titch.

2 I'm Fred.
And I'm Poppy.
I'm Titch!
I'm Titch!

3 Hello children.
Look, Mr Fixit's here.
Hello!
I'm Titch.

4 What's this?
It's my fixit kit.

5

6 I'm Titch.

2 Find and number. Say.

3 Listen again and act. 1.5

1 **Listen and find.** 1.6

2 **Listen and repeat.** 1.7

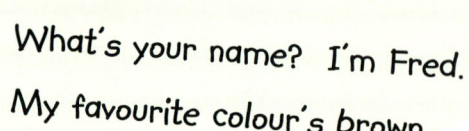

What's your name? I'm Fred.
My favourite colour's brown.

3 **Listen and follow. Say the names.** 1.8 **Listen again and repeat.**

Lesson 5 ▷ AB pages 5–6

What's your name? I'm ... My favourite colour's ...

1 Listen and sing. 🔵 1.14

Shapes

1 Look and say.

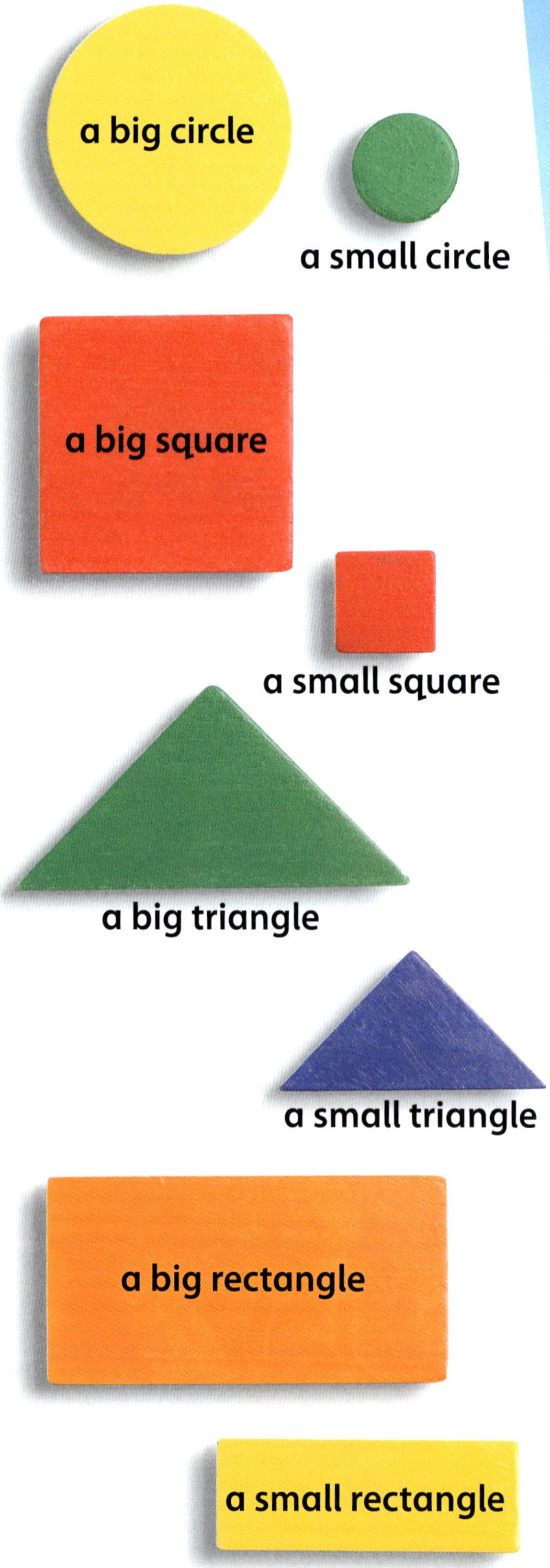

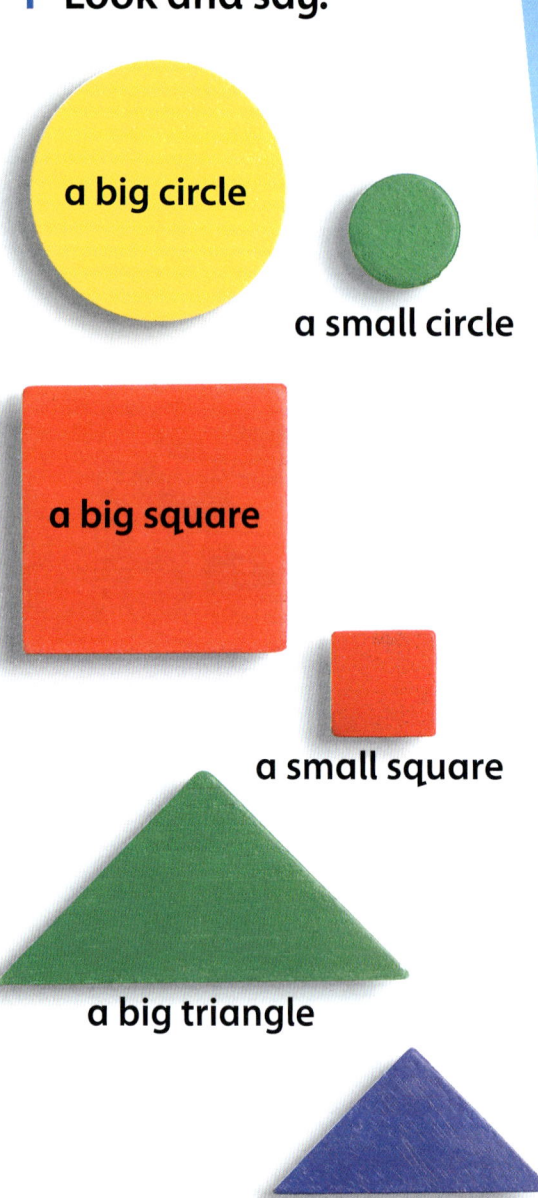

a big circle

a small circle

a big square

a small square

a big triangle

a small triangle

a big rectangle

a small rectangle

2 Listen and find. Count and say. 🎵 1.15

1 Make a shape picture.

Colour.

Cut out.

Stick.

Write.

1 Listen and point. 🔊 1.16 **Listen again and repeat.**

pink
Polly
paint
purple

2 Listen, point and say. 🔊 1.17 **Now it's your turn.**

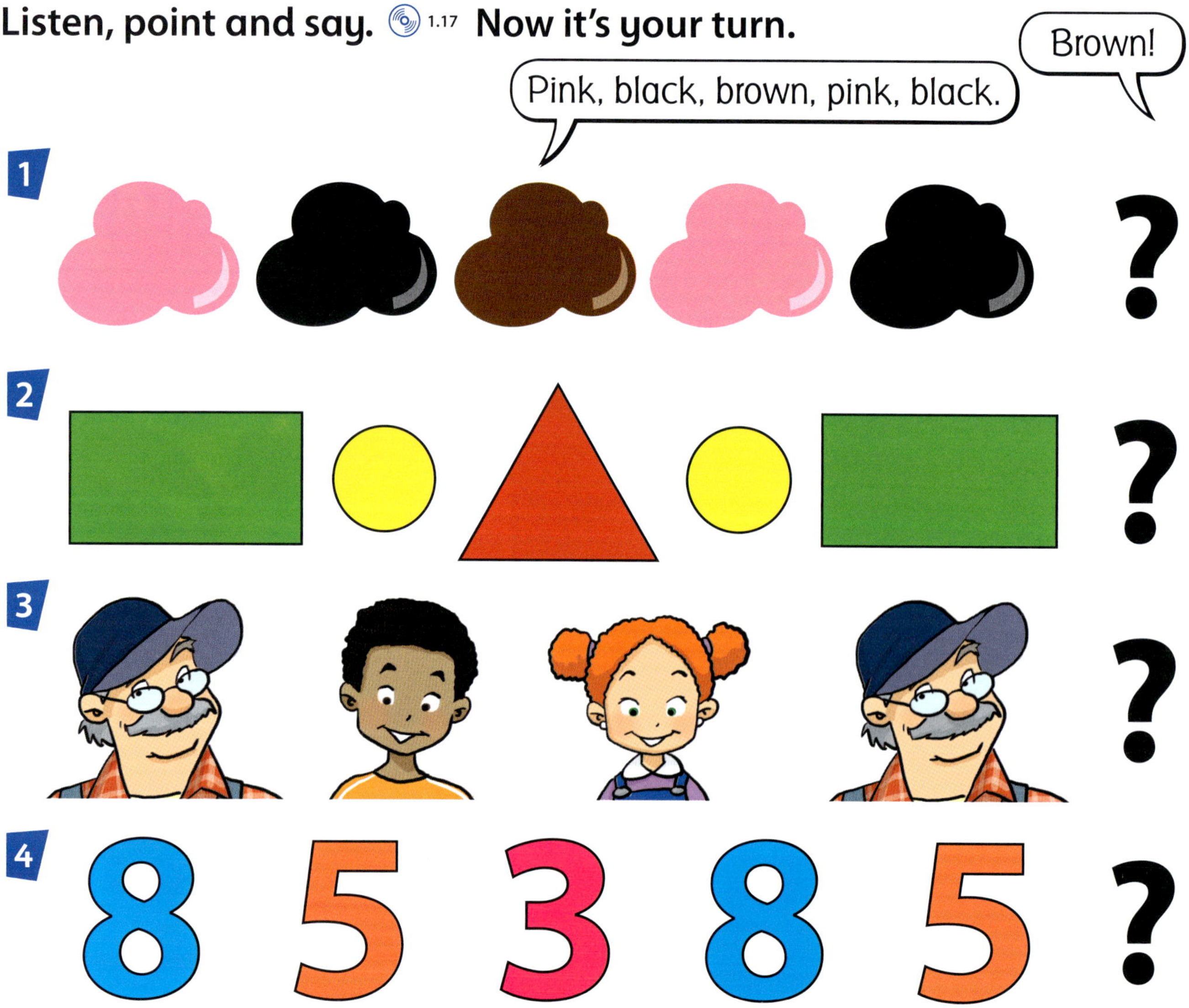

Pink, black, brown, pink, black.

Brown!

1

2

3

4

8 5 3 8 5 ?

2 The school show

1 Look and say. Listen and find. 🎧 1.21
2 Listen and sing. 🎧 1.22

WELCOME TO THE SHOW

Dad Mum

TICKE

Grandpa

Grandma

uncle

sister

aunt

brother

cousin

cousin

1 Listen and point. 🎧 1.26

Abracadabra!

2 Find and number. Say.

3 Listen again and act. 1.26

1 Listen, find and say the numbers. 🔊 1.27
Listen again and repeat.

How old are you?
I'm 6.

Anna, 6

Sam, 8

Katy, 7

Tom, 6

Emily, 7

2 Listen and follow. Say the colour. 🔊 1.28

1 Listen and sing. 🔘 1.31

People and art

1 Look and say.

man

woman

boy

girl

More haste less speed
Arthur John Elsley

Head over tails
(renamed by William
Lever) Dorothy Tennant

2 Listen and find. 🔘 1.33

People

3

The Hornby Train
Claude Maurice Rogers

Family in the Park
Colin Bootman

4

1 Make a picture and a frame.

Colour.

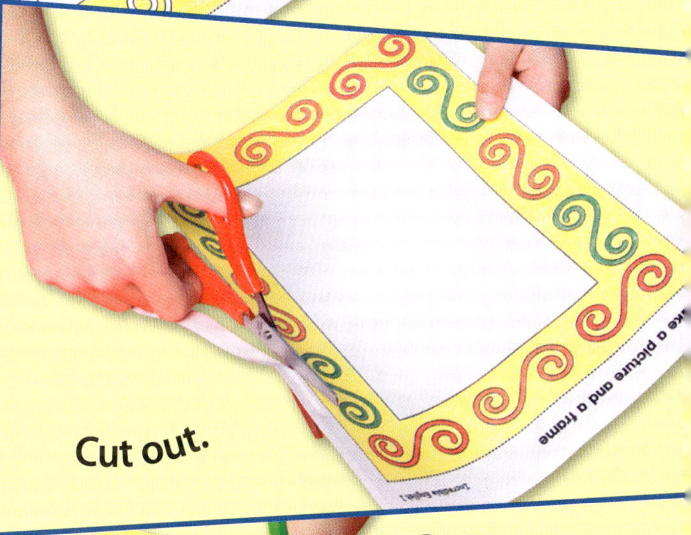

Cut out.

Draw.

Say.

1 Listen and point. 🔘 1.36 **Listen again and repeat.**

six sisters

seven sisters

boy

big book

big boy

book

2 Listen and say the number. 🔘 1.37 **Now it's your turn.**

What's your name?   Emir

How old are you?   7.

Number 3!

1

Sarah 7

2

Dan 6

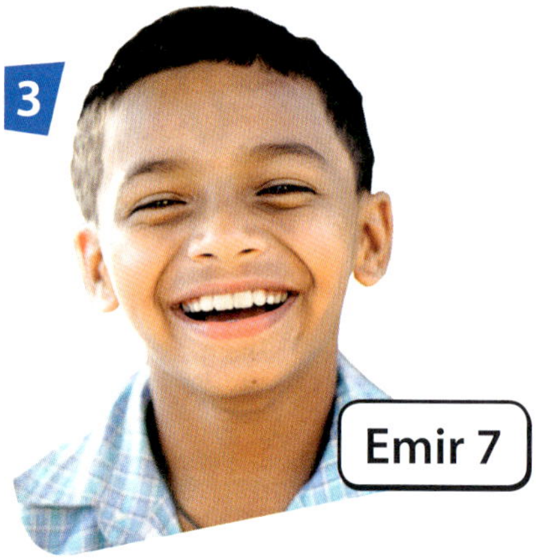

3

Emir 7

Maria 5

4

Ella 6

5

Jacob 8

6

3 The picnic

1 Look and say. Listen and find.  1.41

2 Listen and say. 1.42

chocolate bar

cake

yoghurt

fizzy drink

juice

sandwich

FRED

TITCH

FLO

biscuit

banana

orange

apple

1 Listen and point. 1.46

Naughty Norton!

2 Find and number. Say.

3 Listen again and act. 🎧 1.46

1 **Listen and find the food. Say the names.** 🔊 1.47

I've got an apple!

2 **Listen and say the colours.** 🔊 1.48 **Listen again and repeat.**

I've got a cake. I've got a biscuit.

Red!

Lesson 5 ▷ AB pages 23–24

I've got a banana!

1 Listen and sing. 🎵 1.53

Sugar in food and drink

1 Look and say.

2 Listen and find. Count and say. 🔊 1.55

orange juice

bread roll

chocolate bar

fizzy drink

cereal bar

carrot

banana

apple

milk

yoghurt

cake

biscuits

1 Make a spoon.

Colour.

Cut out.

Stick.

Say.

1 Listen and point. 🔘 1.56 **Listen again and repeat.**

cakes

carrots

cousins

Yum!

yellow

yoghurt

2 Listen and point. 🔘 1.57 **Now it's your turn.**

Me and my world

1 **Read and number.**

2 **Read again, listen and check.** 1.61

☐ Hello! My name's Linda. I'm from Cape Town, in South Africa. I'm six.
I've got a sister. My favourite colour is blue.

☐ Hello! My name's Isabel. I'm from Rio, in Brazil. My favourite colour is red.
I've got a big brother and a big sister. I'm five.

☐ Hello! My name's Haluk. I'm from Istanbul, in Turkey. I've got a little sister.
My favourite colour is orange. I'm six.

☐ Hello! My name's Rebecca. I'm seven. I'm from London, in England.
My favourite colour is purple. I've got a brother.

Revision

Start

Finish

4 The toy cupboard

1 **Look and say. Listen and find.** 2.1

2 **Listen and sing.** 2.2

ball

plane

teddy

car

bike

computer

puppet

robot

train

doll

1 Listen and point. 2.5

Where's my teddy?

6 Here's a ball, and a train ...

And a plane, and a puppet.

Can you see my teddy?

7 Yes! My teddy! It's here!

8 Where's my doll?

I WANT MY DOLL!

2 Find and number. Say.

6

3 Listen again and act. 2.5

1 Listen and find. Say the names. 🔊 2.6

Where's my robot?

It's here. / It isn't here.

2 Listen and tick ✔ or cross ✘. 🔊 2.7 **Listen again and repeat.**

Lesson 5 → AB pages 35–36

Where's my robot? It's here. / It isn't here.

1 Listen and sing. 2.10

What are toys made of?

1 Look and say. **2** Listen and find. 2.12

fabric

It's made of fabric.

wood

It's made of wood.

Materials

plastic

5

International Air

It's made of plastic.

9

3

TGV EXPRESS

metal

13

It's made of metal.

1 Make a spinner.

Draw and colour.

plastic

fabric

wood

Cut out.

metal · plastic · fabric

Put it together.

wood

Play.

1 Listen and point. 🎧 2.15 Listen again and repeat.

red robot   plastic plane

2 Listen and follow. 🎧 2.16 Now it's your turn.

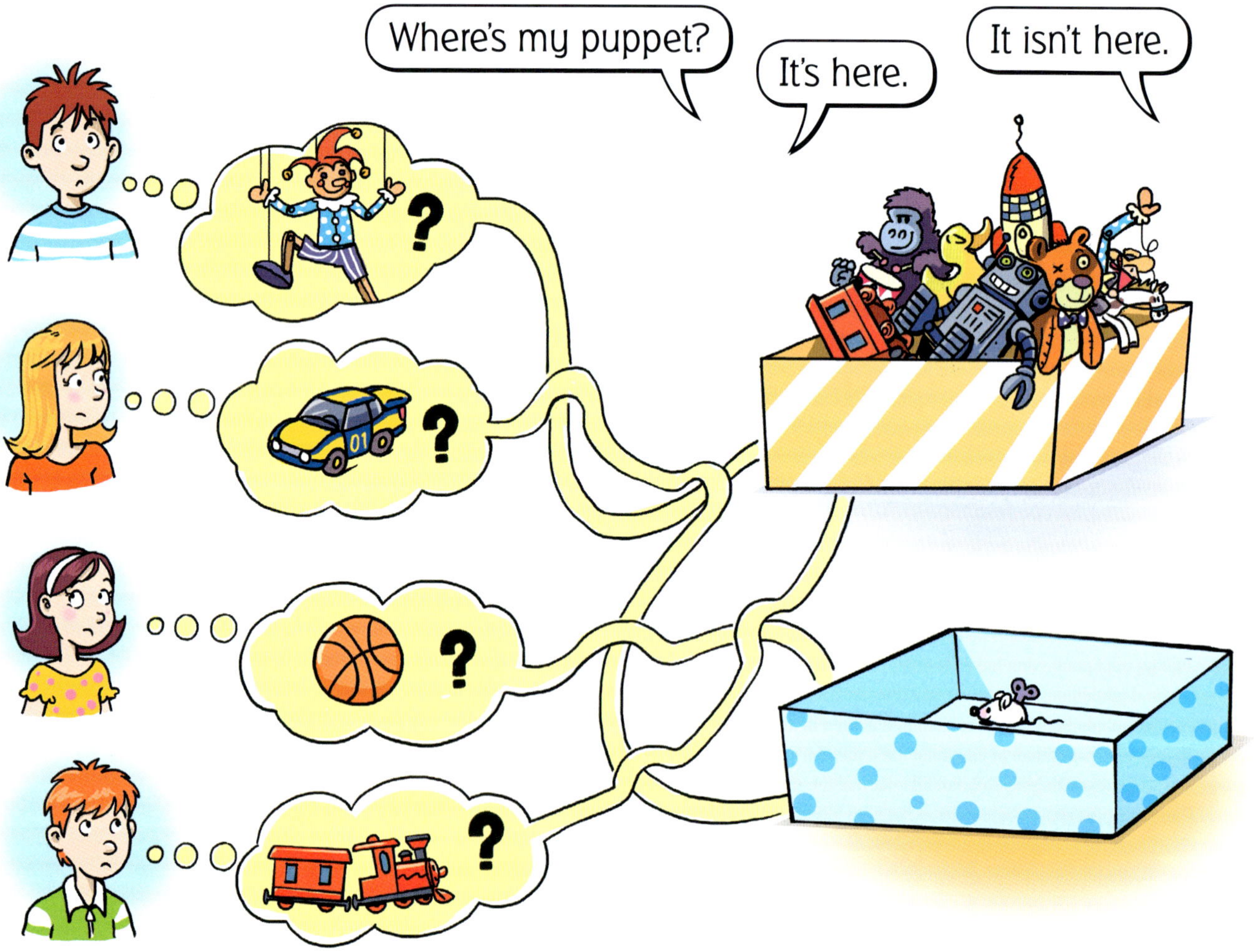

Where's my puppet?   It's here.   It isn't here.

5 Puppets

1 Look and say. Listen and find. 🔊 2.18
2 Listen and sing. 🔊 2.19

head

hands

fingers

arms

body

toes

legs

feet

1 Listen and point. 2.21

2 Find and number. Say.

3 Listen again and act. 2.21

1 Listen and say *True* or *False*.  2.22

It's got a big head.

It's got three arms.

2 Listen and say the number. 2.23

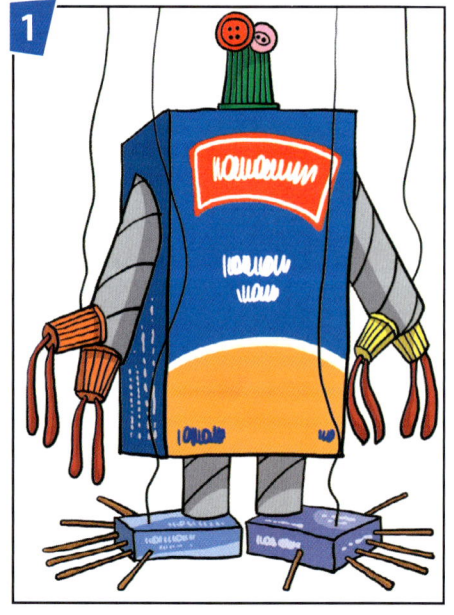

It's got a big head.

1 Listen and sing. 2.26

Song

Block graphs

1 Look and say.

2 Listen and find. 2.27

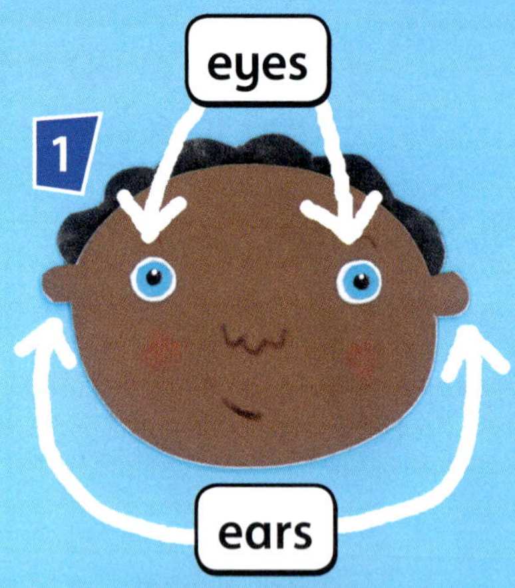

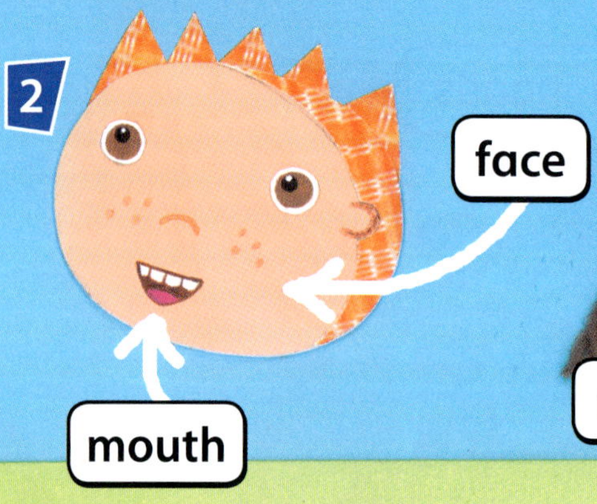

eyes

1

ears

face

2

mouth

3

hair

nose

brown eyes

6

red hair

7

Hair colour in class 1

blue eyes

8

brown hair

9

green eyes

10

Parts of the face

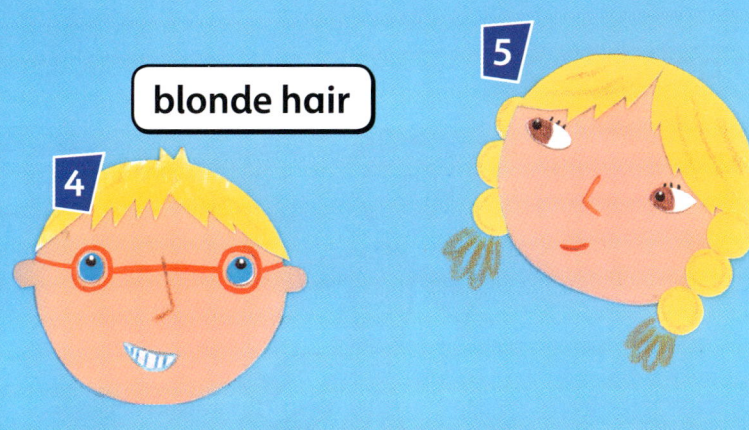

blonde hair

4

5

Eye colour in class 1

11

12

black hair

1 Make paper people.

Fold.

Cut out.

Draw and colour.

Say.

1 Listen and point. 🔘 2.28 Listen again and repeat.

Hello!

hands   head   hair

five fingers   four feet

2 Listen and say the number. 🔘 2.29 Now it's your turn.

It's got black hair and blue eyes.
It's got red arms and blue legs.

Number 1!

1

2

3

4

6 At the farm

1 Look and say. Listen and find. 🔊 2.31
2 Listen and sing. 🔊 2.32

donkey

dog

cat

duck

rabbit

horse

goat

cow

hen

sheep

1 Listen and point. 2.35

Animals

2 Find and number. Say.

3

3 Listen again and act. 🎧 2.35

1 **Listen, find and say the names.** 🎧 2.36
Listen again and repeat.

I like ducks.
I don't like sheep.

2 **Listen and follow. Say who.** 🎧 2.37

Lesson 5 ➤ AB pages 53–54

I like ducks. I don't like sheep.

1 Listen and sing. 🎧 2.40

Baby animals

1 Look and say. **2 Listen and find.** 🔊 2.42

1 kitten

cat

2 hen

chick

4 horse

foal

3

dog

puppy

5

sheep

lamb

1 Make an animal book.

Colour.

Write.

Fold.

Say.

1 Listen and point. 2.44 **Listen again and repeat.**

donkey

Dad

chocolate

chick

chair

duck

2 Listen and say who. 2.45 **Now it's your turn.**

I don't like puppies.
I like goats.

You're Maria!

 Jacob	🙂	☹️	☹️	🙂
 Dan	🙂	🙂	☹️	🙂
 Maria	☹️	🙂	🙂	☹️
 Ella	☹️	☹️	🙂	☹️

Me and my world

1 Read and number.

2 Read again, listen and check. 🎧 2.47

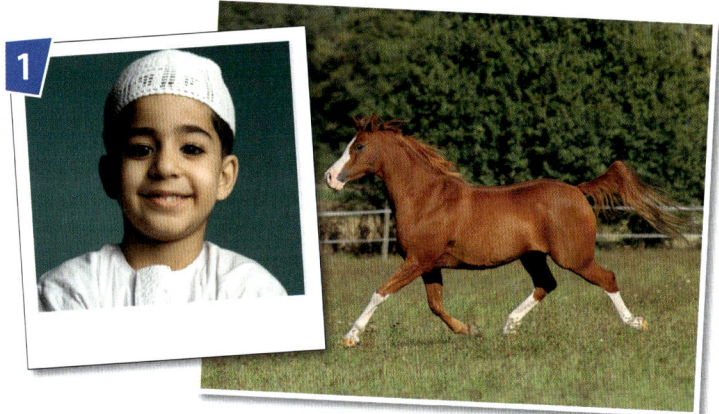

☐ Hello! My name's Li. I'm from China. This is a Mandarin duck. It's from China too. It's my favourite animal. You can *see* Mandarin ducks in zoos and parks.

☐ Hi! I'm Sally. I'm from Canada. I like dogs, they are my favourite animal. My dog is black and white. She's got blue eyes.

☐ Hello! My name's Caleb. I'm from Dubai. I love horses. I've got a horse. He's brown and he's got a white nose. He's got a long brown tail too.

☐ Hello! I'm Meg. I'm from Scotland. This is my cow, Mabel and her calf, Toby. Mabel has got long hair and very long horns! Toby is one, he's sweet!

Start

Finish

7 | At the park

1 Look and say. Listen and find. 🔘 2.50

2 Listen and say. 🔘 2.51

ride a bike

kick a ball

walk

throw a frisbee

hop

juggle

fly

jump

climb a tree

run

Actions

Lesson 2 ▶ AB pages 62–63

1 **Listen and point.**  2.54

Playing in the park

6 Just the thing! A trampoline!

Jump!

7 You can do it!

Jump! Jump!

Well done!

8 Oh!

Oooh!

HELP!

2 Find and number. Say.

1

3 Listen again and act. 🎧 2.54

1 **Listen, find and say the names.** 🔊 2.55
   Listen again and repeat.

I can climb. I can't juggle.
Can you fly? Yes / No.

2 **Listen and follow. Say** *Yes* **or** *No.* 🔊 2.56

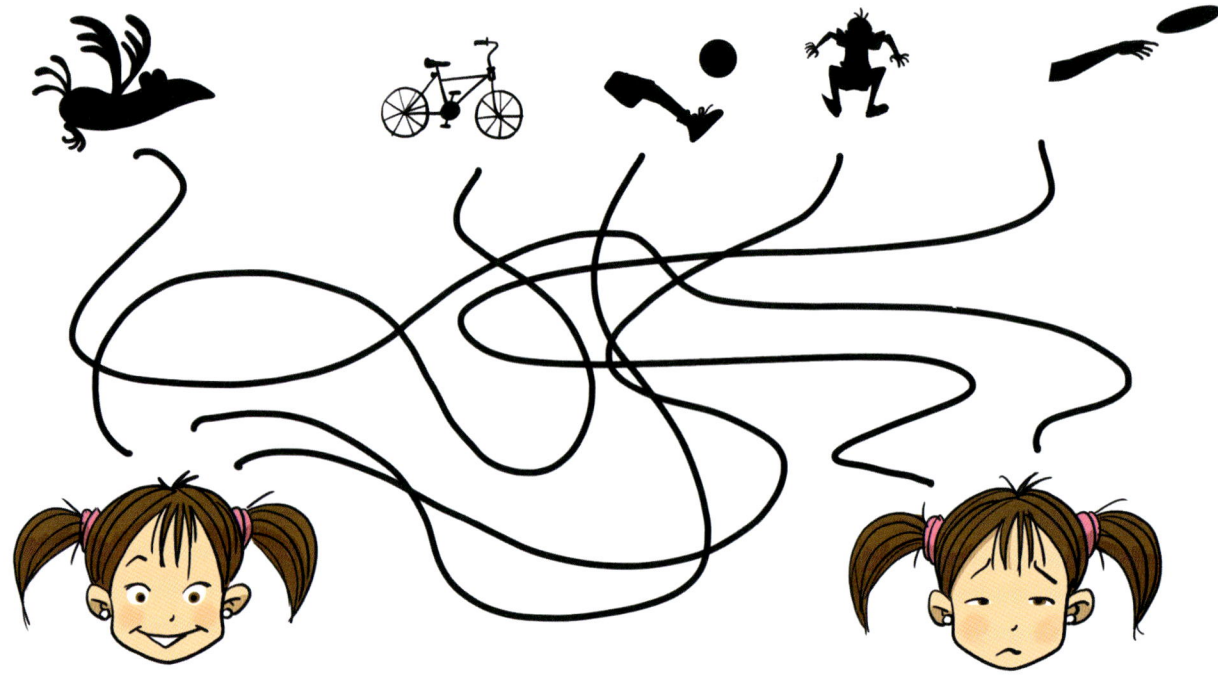

Lesson 5 ➡ AB pages 65–66

I can / I can't fly. Can you fly? Yes. / No.

1 Listen and sing. 2.59

Growing up

1 Look and say.

walk

read

write

talk

draw

swim

2 Listen, find and say. 2.60

I'm 1.

I'm 4.

Abilities

I'm 5.

I'm 7.

1 Make a photo album.

Draw and colour.

Write.

Fold.

Say.

1 Listen and point. 🔊 2.62 **Listen again and repeat.**

read   run   **w**oods   **w**here   **w**alk

2 Ask and answer.

Can you ride a bike?   Yes.   No.

8 New clothes

1 Look and say. Listen and find. 🎧 3.1

2 Listen and sing. 💿 3.2

hat

socks

T-shirt

jumper

skirt

jacket

dress

trousers

shorts

shoes

1 Listen and point. 3.5

6 What's in my kit today? Let's see ...

socks ...

shoes ...

a hat ...

7 ... and a big red nose!

8 Look! I'm a clown! Perfect for a party!

2 Find and number. Say.

3

I'm 7

3 Listen again and act. 3.5

1 Listen and follow. Say the names. 3.6
Listen again and repeat.

I'm wearing a grey T-shirt.

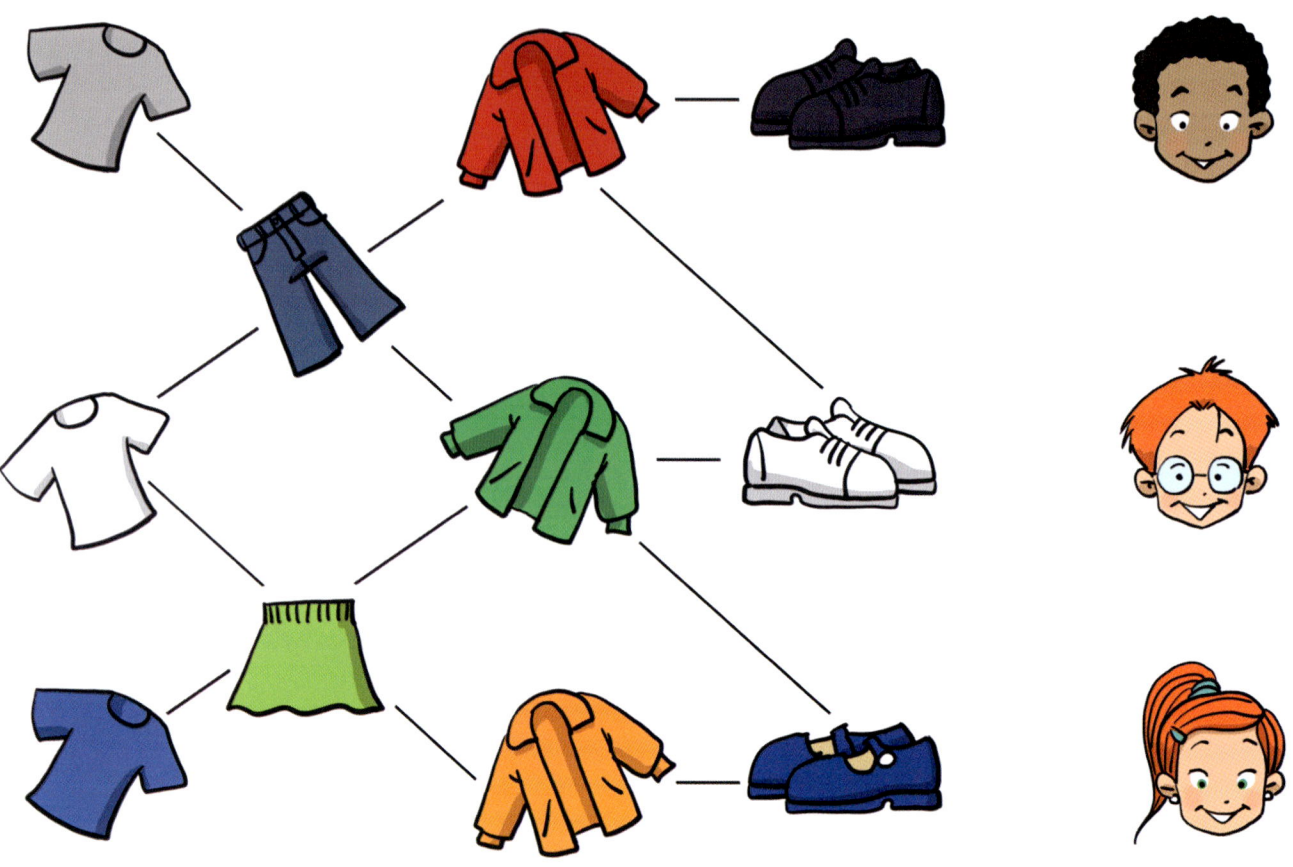

2 Listen and say *True* or *False*. 3.7

Lesson 5 ▷ AB pages 74–75

I'm wearing a grey T-shirt.

1 Listen and sing. 🔊 3.10

Song

Stamp your feet!

Clap your hands!

Slap your legs!

Tap your nose!

The weather in art

1 **Look and say.**   **2** **Listen, find and say.** 🔊 3.12

It's raining.

It's cloudy.

It's cold.

1	*Bridge, Sudden Shower at Atake* **Ando Hiroshige**
2	*Clouds* **Thomas Cooper Gotch**
3	*Wind* **Georges Barbier**
4	*Bitter Cold* **Dale William Nichols**
5	*The Sun* **Edvard Munch**

Weather

3

It's windy.

5

It's hot.

1 Make a weather mobile.

Colour and write.

Cut out.

Fold and stick.

Say.

1 Listen and point. 3.13 **Listen again and repeat.**

she   shoes   shorts   Joe   jacket   jumper

2 Listen and find. 3.14 **Now it's your turn.**

> I'm wearing a pink jumper and black shoes. I'm wearing blue trousers.

9 House and home

1 Look and say. Listen and find. 🔊 3.16
2 Listen and say. 🔊 3.17

bedroom

bathroom

garage

living room

hall

kitchen

garden

1 Listen and point. 3.20

Norton's missing!

Norton's missing! Is he here?

Let's look.

Look. He's in the kitchen.

That's not Norton!

Oh dear!

Look. He's in the bathroom.

That's not Norton!

Oh no!

I can see Norton in the garden. Look!

2 Find and number. Say.

3 Listen again and act. 3.20

1 Listen and say the names. 🔊 3.21
Listen again and repeat.

2 Listen and answer the questions. 🔊 3.22

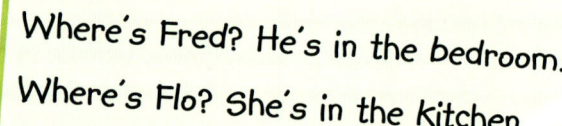
Where's Fred? He's in the bedroom.
Where's Flo? She's in the kitchen.

Lesson 5 ▶ AB pages 83–84

Where's... ? He/She's in the kitchen.

1 Listen and sing. 3.24

Maps

1 Look and say.

2 Listen, find and say. 🔊 3.26

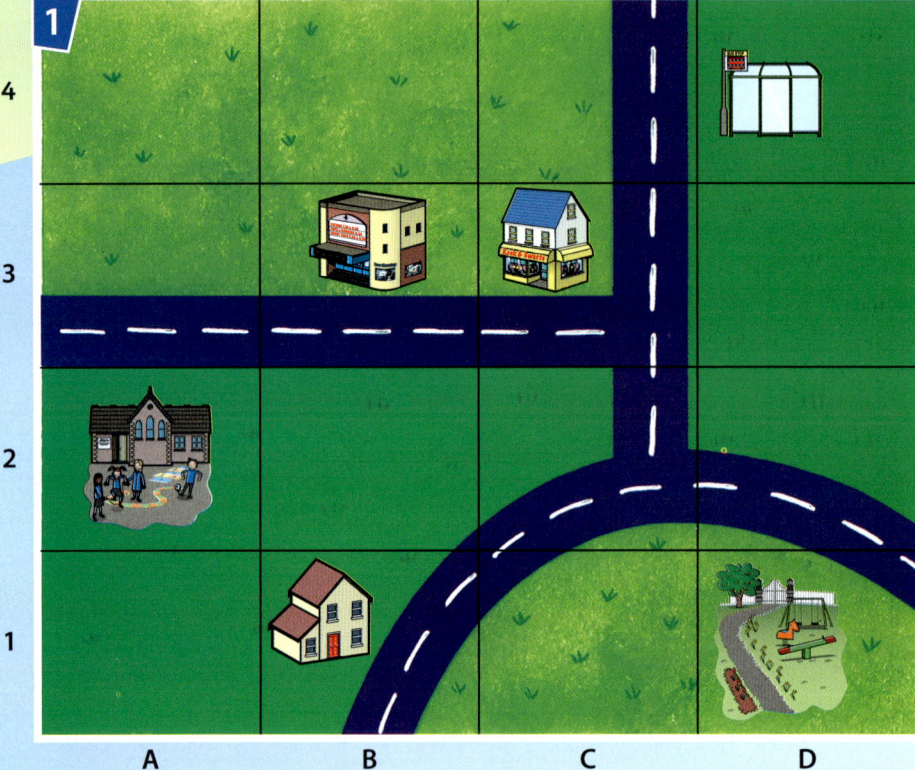

park

shop

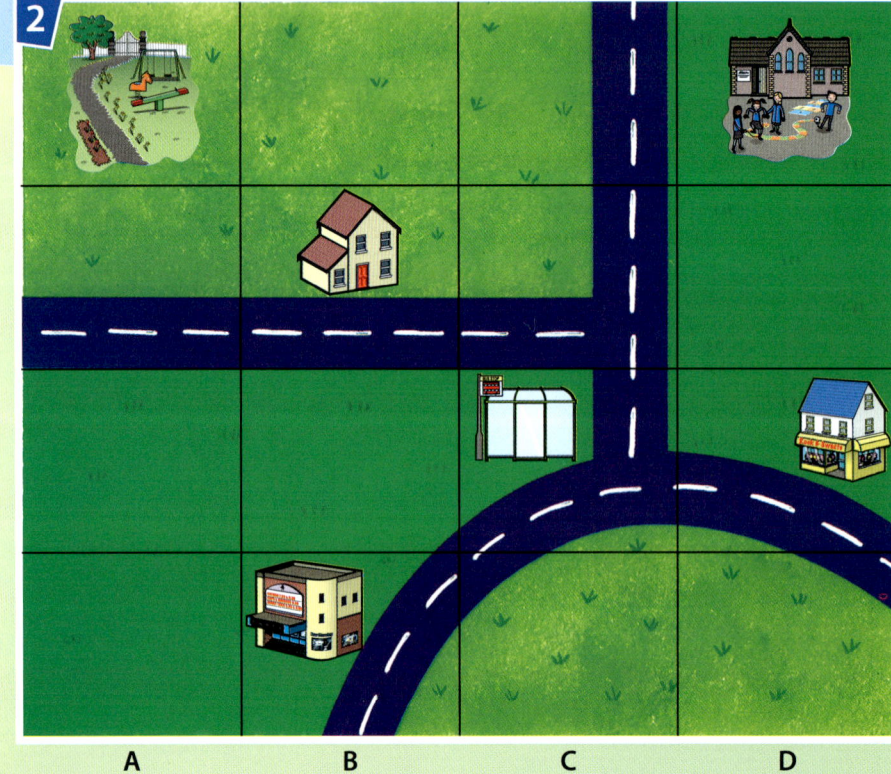

bus stop

Places in a town

school

cinema

house

1 Make a house.

Colour.

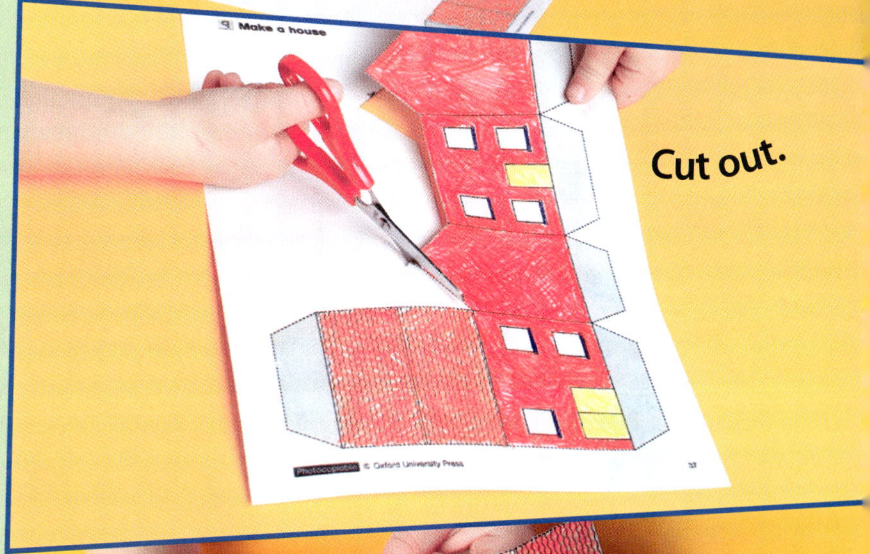

Cut out.

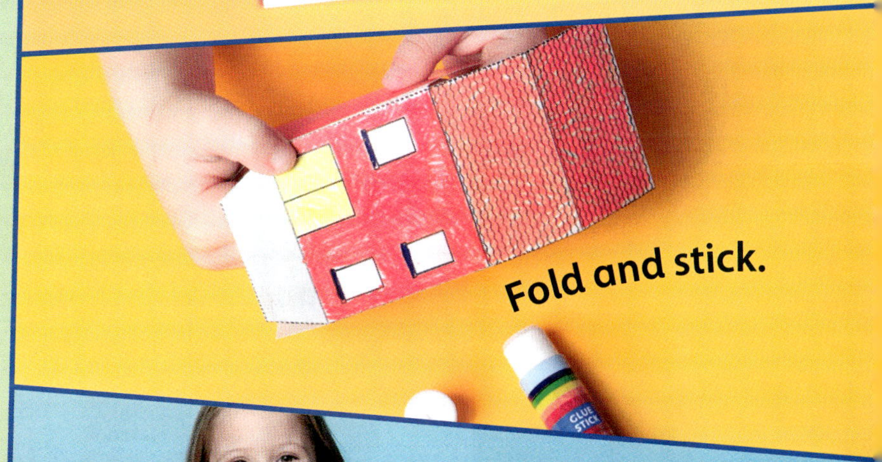

Fold and stick.

Make a street.

1 Listen and point. 🔘 3.27 **Listen again and repeat.**

garage

girl

goat   **g**arden

lamb   **l**iving room

2 Listen and answer. 🔘 3.28 **Now it's your turn.**

Where's Dad?

He's in the garden.

Dad

Mum

Grandma

Grandpa

Ava

Maisy

Luke

Alex

Me and my world

1 Read and number.
2 Read again, listen and check. 3.30

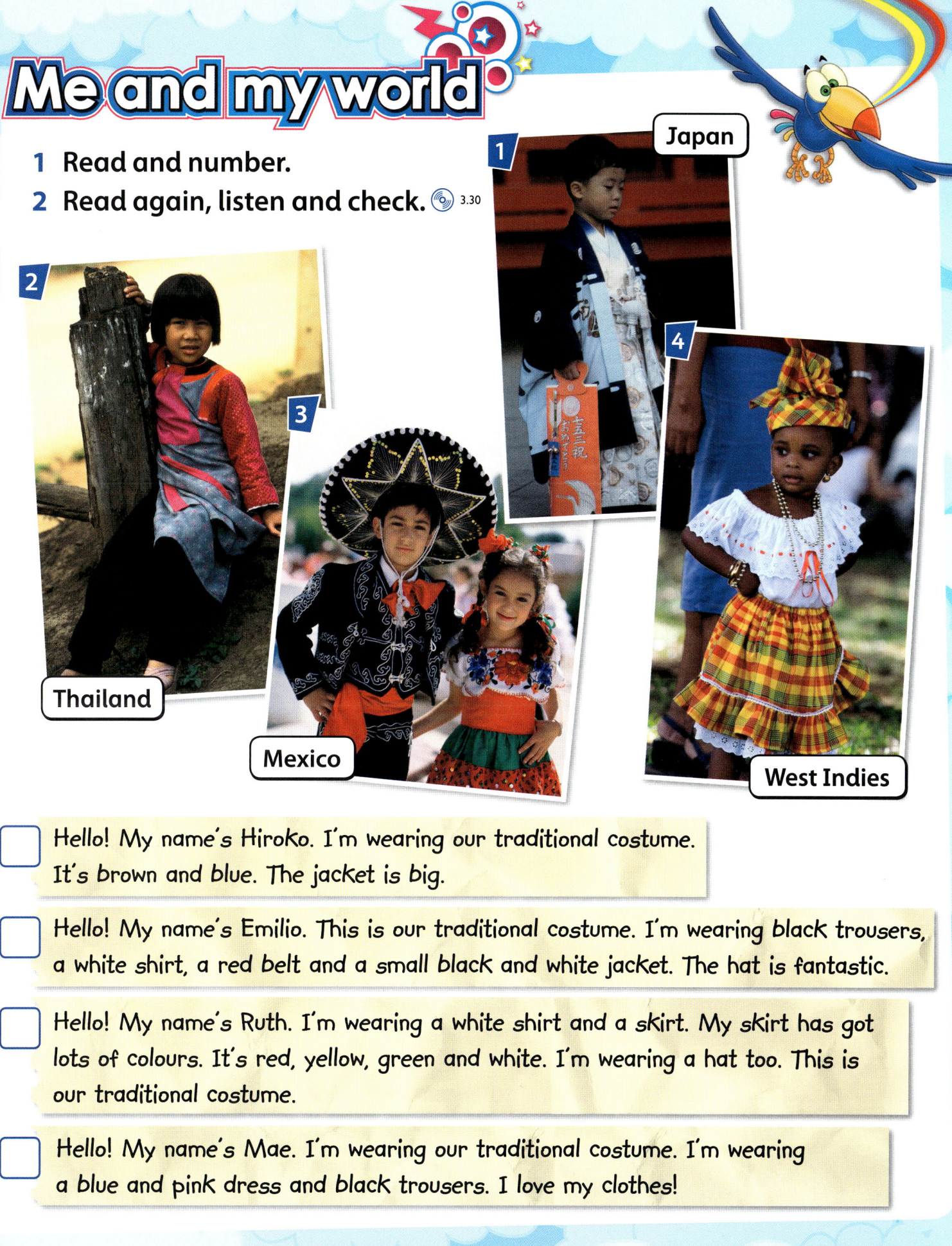

Japan 1

Thailand 2

Mexico 3

West Indies 4

Hello! My name's Hiroko. I'm wearing our traditional costume. It's brown and blue. The jacket is big.

Hello! My name's Emilio. This is our traditional costume. I'm wearing black trousers, a white shirt, a red belt and a small black and white jacket. The hat is fantastic.

Hello! My name's Ruth. I'm wearing a white shirt and a skirt. My skirt has got lots of colours. It's red, yellow, green and white. I'm wearing a hat too. This is our traditional costume.

Hello! My name's Mae. I'm wearing our traditional costume. I'm wearing a blue and pink dress and black trousers. I love my clothes!

Start

Finish

Happy Peace Day!

1 Read. Look at the picture and say what's missing.

red **yellow** **blue** **violet**
orange **green** **indigo**

2 Listen and find the colours. 🎧 3.33

Happy Christmas!

1 Listen and find the cards. Say the numbers. 3.34

1 robin bell

2 tree

3 star angel

4

5 candle

2 Listen and sing. 3.35

Happy Mother's Day!

1 Listen and find. 3.36

2 Listen, find and say the names. 3.37

Songs and chants

Unit 1

Page 3 1.2

Stand up, Fred,
Stand up, Flo,
Stand up, Bing ... OK!
Stand up, Poppy,
Stand up, Titch,
Now let me hear you say ... hello!

Page 7 1.14

Listen children, stand up now,
Stand up now, stand up now,
Listen children, stand up now,
Are you ready? Shh shh.

Listen children, sit down now,
Sit down now, sit down now,
Listen children, sit down now,
Are you ready? Shh shh.

Listen children, line up now,
Line up now, line up now,
Listen children, line up now,
Are you ready? Shh shh.

Listen children, say goodbye,
Say goodbye, say goodbye,
Listen children, say goodbye,
Are you ready? Shh shh.

Unit 2

Page 11 1.21

Aunt and uncle, aunt and uncle,
Dad and Mum, Dad and Mum,
Brother, sister, cousin,
Brother, sister, cousin,
In row one, in row one.

Page 15 1.31

The curtains at the show go swish ... swish,
Swish ... swish, swish ... swish.
The curtains at the show go swish ... swish,
All night long.

The Mums at the show all clap their hands,
Clap their hands, clap their hands.
The Mums at the show all clap their hands,
All night long.

The Dads at the show say Good luck, kids!
Good luck, kids! Good luck, kids!
The Dads at the show say Good luck, kids!
All night long.

The uncles at the show say Well done, kids!
Well done, kids! Well done, kids!
The uncles at the show say Well done, kids!
All night long.

The aunts at the show say Very good!
Very good! Very good!
The aunts at the show say Very good!
All night long.

The curtains at the show go swish ... swish,
Swish ... swish, swish ... swish.
The curtains at the show go swish ... swish,
All night long.

Unit 3

Page 19 1.42

Apples, apples,
Juice and yoghurt, juice and yoghurt,
Biscuits and cakes, biscuits and cakes,
Oranges and chocolate bars,
Oranges and chocolate bars,
Fizzy drinks, fizzy drinks, fizzy drinks,
Whoosh!

1.53

Time for tea, time for tea,
Wash your hands, it's time for tea.
I've got a sandwich, I've got juice.
I've got an apple and a chocolate mousse!

Show me your hands now.
What dirty hands!
Show me your hands now.
What dirty hands!

Time for tea, time for tea,
Wash your hands, it's time for tea.
I've got a sandwich, I've got juice.
I've got an apple and a chocolate mousse!

Show me your hands now.
What clean hands!
Show me your hands now.
What clean hands!

Time for tea, time for tea,
Come and eat, it's time for tea!

Unit 4

  2.2

Doll, robot, car and train, car and train,
Doll, robot, car and train, car and train,
Bike and ball and teddy and plane,
Doll, robot, car and train, car and train.

  2.10

Come and share a toy with me,
Come and share a toy with me.
Your turn, my turn,
Come and share a toy with me.

Come and sing a song with me,
Come and sing a song with me.
Your turn, my turn,
Come and sing a song with me.

Come and read a book with me,
Come and read a book with me.
Your turn, my turn,
Come and read a book with me.

Come and play a game with me,
Come and play a game with me.
Your turn, my turn,
Come and play a game with me.

Unit 5

2.19

Fingers, hands, keep moving,
Fingers, hands, keep moving,
Fingers, hands, keep moving,
We're puppets in a show!

Fingers, hands, feet, keep moving,
Fingers, hands, feet, keep moving,
Fingers, hands, feet, keep moving,
We're puppets in a show!

Fingers, hands, feet, head, keep moving,
Fingers, hands, feet, head, keep moving,
Fingers, hands, feet, head, keep moving,
We're puppets in a show!

Page 41 2.26

Clap your hands,
Clap your hands,
Stretch up high and touch the sky,
And clap your hands.

Clap in twos,
Clap in twos,
Stetch up high and touch the sky,
And clap in twos.

Clap in fours,
Clap in fours,
Stretch up high and touch the sky,
And clap in fours.

Unit 6

Page 45 2.32

I've got a cow and a sheep on my farm,
I've got a cow and a sheep on my farm,
I've got a cow and a sheep on my farm,
And I've got a donkey.

I've got a dog and a cat on my farm,
I've got a dog and a cat on my farm,
I've got a dog and a cat on my farm,
And I've got a donkey.

I've got a duck and a hen on my farm,
I've got a duck and a hen on my farm,
I've got a duck and a hen on my farm,
And I've got a donkey.

Page 45 2.64

I've got a moo and a baa on my farm,
I've got a moo and a baa on my farm,
I've got a moo and a baa on my farm,
And I've got an ee-aw.

I've got a woof and a miaow on my farm,
I've got a woof and a miaow on my farm,
I've got a woof and a miaow on my farm,
And I've got an ee-aw.

I've got a quack and a cluck on my farm,
I've got a quack and a cluck on my farm,
I've got a quack and a cluck on my farm,
And I've got an ee-aw.

Page 49 2.40

I've got a dog, I've got a dog,
Come here, good boy,
I've got a dog.

Let's feed the dog, let's feed the dog,
Come here, good boy,
Let's feed the dog.

Let's brush the dog, let's brush the dog,
Come here, good boy,
Let's brush the dog.

Let's walk the dog, let's walk the dog,
Come here, good boy,
Let's walk the dog.

Let's stroke the dog, let's stroke the dog,
Come here, good boy,
Let's stroke the dog.

Unit 7

Page 55 2.51

Hop, hop, hop. Hop, hop, hop!
One, two, three. Look at me!

Run, run, run. Run, run, run!
One, two, three. Look at me!

Jump, jump, jump. Jump, jump, jump!
One, two, three. Look at me!

Fly, fly, fly. Fly, fly, fly!
One, two, three. Look at me!

Stop now please. Stop now please!
Three, two, one. That was fun!

Page 59

 2.59

Exercise is lots of fun,
You can walk or you can run.
Kick a ball, climb a tree,
Ride a bike or hop like me!

Jump, jump, jump, up and down!
Touch your toes and turn around!
Jump, jump, jump, up and down!
Touch your toes and turn around!

Exercise is lots of fun,
You can walk or you can run.
Kick a ball, climb a tree,
Ride a bike or hop like me!

Unit 8

Page 63

 3.2

I've got shoes and socks,
I've got trousers too,
Jumper, hat, skirt and dress,
Clothes for me and you.

Page 67

 3.10

Stamp your feet, stamp your feet,
If you're wearing something BLUE!
If you're wearing something blue.

Clap your hands, clap your hands,
If you're wearing something RED!
If you're wearing something red.

Slap your legs, slap your legs,
If you're wearing something GREEN!
If you're wearing something green.

Tap your nose, tap your nose,
If you're wearing something BLACK!
If you're wearing something black.

Unit 9

Page 71

 3.17

Knock, knock, knock,
Run and hide.
Knock, knock, knock,
Look inside.
Bathroom, bedroom, kitchen, where?
Living room, garage ... You're in there!

Page 75

 3.24

We're in the kitchen, washing up,
We're in the kitchen, washing up,
We're in the kitchen, washing up,
Washing up together!

We're in the bedroom, tidying up,
We're in the bedroom, tidying up,
We're in the bedroom, tidying up,
Tidying up together!

We're in the bathroom, cleaning up,
We're in the bathroom, cleaning up,
We're in the bathroom, cleaning up,
Cleaning up together!

Everything is tidy. We can play!
Everything is tidy. We can play!
Everything is tidy. We can play!
We can play together!

Page 82

 3.35

Stars and bells, stars and bells,
Robins and a tree.
Here's a card on Christmas Day,
With love to you from me!

Oh! Stars and bells, stars and bells,
Robins and a tree.
Here's a card on Christmas Day,
With love to you from me!

Let's practise!

1 Look, read and circle. There is one example.

1

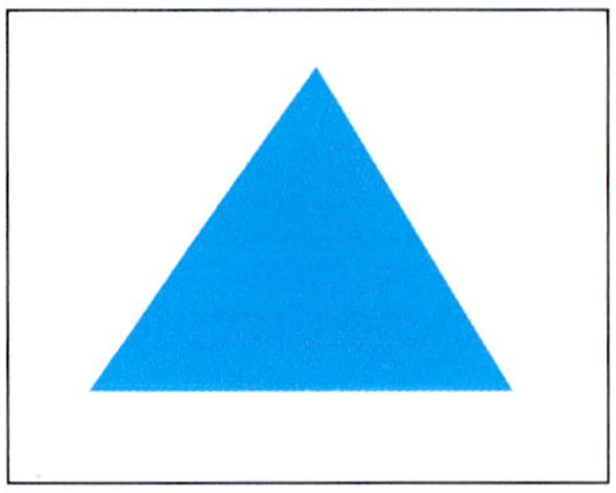

a square	(a triangle)	a circle

2

an orange	a yoghurt	a banana

3

a woman	a man	a girl

4

a cake	a sandwich	a biscuit

5

a fizzy drink	an apple	a carrot

6

a man	a girl	a boy

Starters Reading & Writing

Look and read. Put a (✔) or a cross (✘) in the box.
There are two examples.

Examples

This is a triangle.   ✔

This is a fizzy drink.   ✘

Questions

1
This is a girl.   ☐

2
This is an apple.   ☐

3
This is a banana.   ☐

4
This is a yoghurt.   ☐

5
This is a woman.   ☐

Let's practise!

1 Listen and write the numbers. There is one example. 🔘 3.38

2 Listen and colour. There is one example. 🔘 3.39

Starters Listening

Listen and colour. There is one example. 🔊 3.40

Starters — Let's practise!

1 Listen and point to the things in the picture. 🔊 3.41

2 Look, listen and answer. There is one example. 🔊 3.42

1

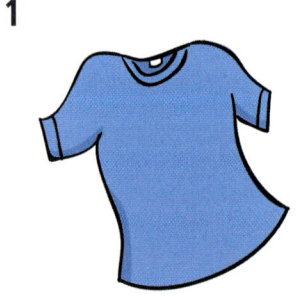

2

3

4

5

6

Starters Speaking

Listen and point to the things in the picture. 🔊 3.43

Point to the things in the picture. Ask and answer.

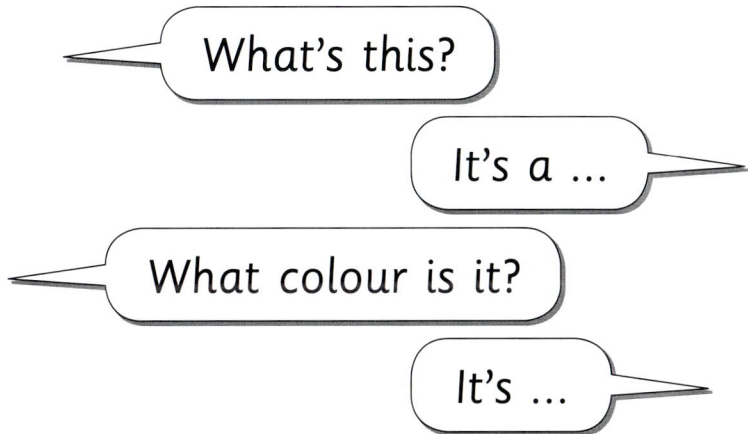

What's this?

It's a ...

What colour is it?

It's ...

1 Look at the pictures and read the words.
Look at the letters. Draw lines. There is one example.

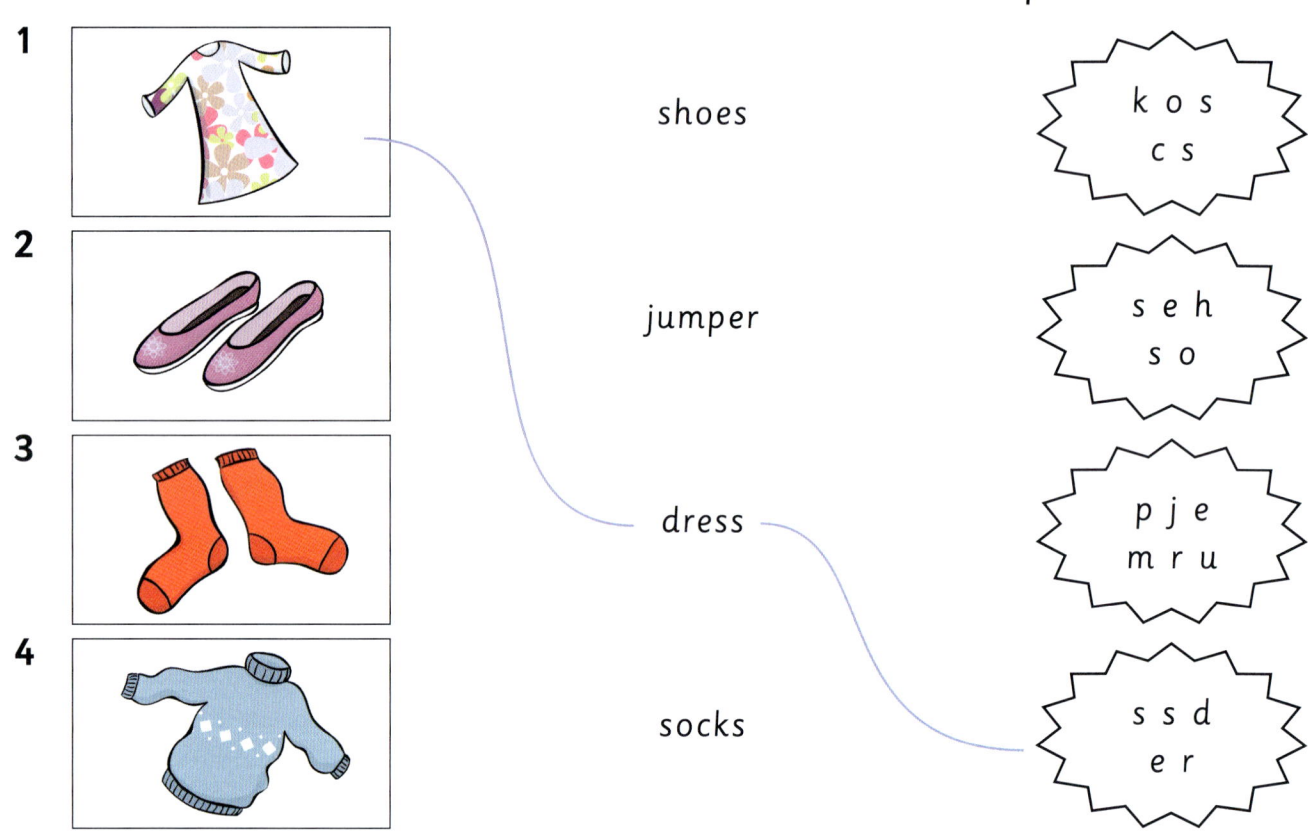

1 shoes — k o s c s

2 jumper — s e h s o

3 dress — p j e m r u

4 socks — s s d e r

2 Look at the pictures. Look at the letters.
Complete the words. There is one example.

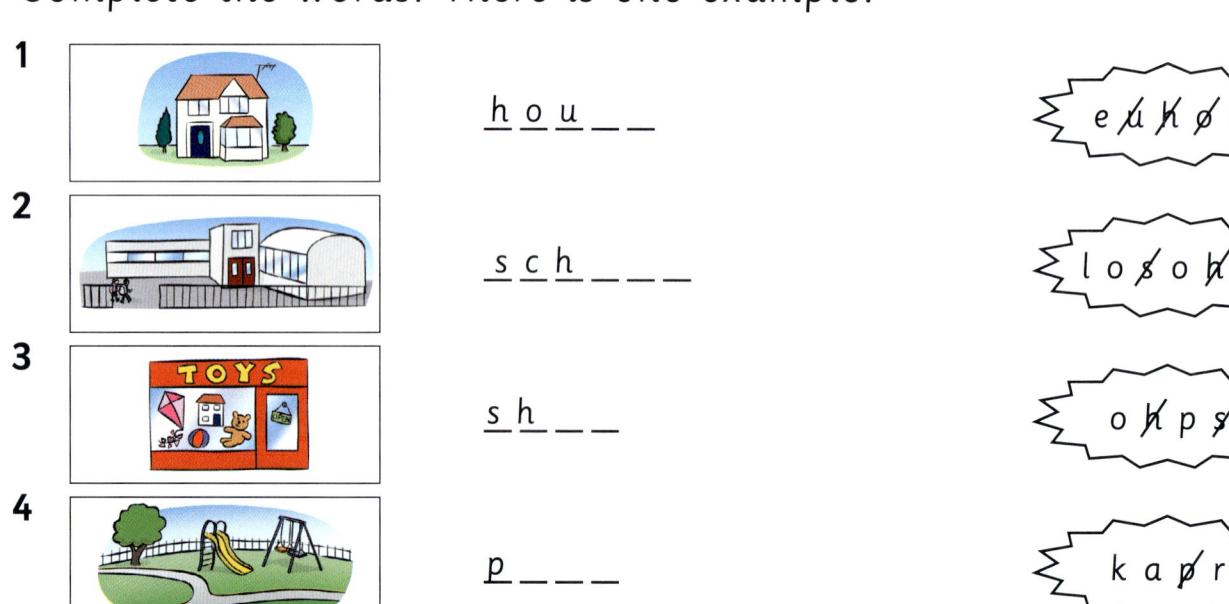

1 h o u _ _ — e u h o s

2 s c h _ _ _ — l o o o k o

3 s h _ _ _ — o k p y

4 p _ _ _ _ — k a p r

Starters Reading & Writing

Look at the pictures. Look at the letters.
Write the words. There is one example.

Example

m o u t h

t u m
o h

Questions

1

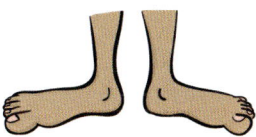

_ _ _ _

e f
t e

2

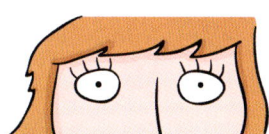

_ _ _ _

y s
e e

3

_ _ _ _

m r
s a

4

_ _ _ _

s e
n o

5

_ _ _ _

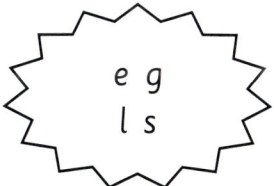

e g
l s

OXFORD
UNIVERSITY PRESS

Great Clarendon Street, Oxford, OX2 6DP, United Kingdom

Oxford University Press is a department of the University of Oxford.
It furthers the University's objective of excellence in research, scholarship,
and education by publishing worldwide. Oxford is a registered trade
mark of Oxford University Press in the UK and in certain other countries

© Oxford University Press 2011

The moral rights of the author have been asserted

First published in 2011

2023
16

No unauthorized photocopying

ISBN: 978 0 19 444228 2

Printed in China

This book is printed on paper from certified and well-managed sources

ACKNOWLEDGEMENTS

Main illustrations by: Gustavo Mazali.

Other illustrations by: Beccy Blake pp.7, 15, 23, 33, 41, 49, 59, 60–61, 67, 75;
Judy Brown pp.88, 89, 90, 91, 92, 93, 94, 95; John Haslam pp.28, 54, 80; Maria
Maddocks/The Organisation pp.42–43; Dusan Pavlic/Beehive Illustration
pp.26 (bottom), 36 (bottom), 44 (bottom); Andres Martinez Ricci/The
Organisation pp.10 (top), 18 (top), 26 (top), 36 (top), 44 (top), 52 (top), 62 (top),
70, 78; Mark Ruffle pp.24–25 (sugar spoons), 76.

Cover by: Gustavo Mazali.

Commissioned photography by: Gareth Boden pp.9, 17, 25, 35, 43, 51, 61, 69, 77;
Phil James pp.8–9 (shapes), 34–35; MM Studios pp.24–25, 34–35.

*The Publishers would also like to thank the following for their kind permission to reproduce
photographs and other copyright material*: Akg-images p.69 (Wind/Georges Barbier/
1925); Alamy pp.18 (Emir/Michael Prince/Corbis Flirt, Jacob/Ken Gillespie
Photography, Dan and Sarah/Myrleen Pearson, Maria/Heide Benser/Corbis Cusp),
27 (Rebecca/Alex Segre, Haluk/Ronnie Kaufman/Corbis Bridge), 52 (Jacob/Ken
Gillespie Photography, Dan/Myrleen Pearson, Maria/Heide Benser/Corbis
Cusp, puppies/PVStock.com), 62 (ride a bike/Dennis MacDonald), 76 (shop/
Robert Slade/Manor Photography, bus stop/Jeff Morgan 02), 77 (cinema/Tracey
Fahy, house/Robert Brook/Photofusion Picture Library); 79 (Mae/Anders Ryman/
Corbis Nomad, Emilio/Jon Arnold Images Ltd, Ruth/Scot T. Smith/Danita
Delimont, Agent, Hiroko/Tibor Bognar); Ardea pp.50 (chicken/John Daniels,
horse/Arco Images GmbH), 51 (dog/Jean Michel Labat); The Bridgeman Art
Library pp.16 (*More Haste Less Speed*, 1899, Elsley, Arthur John (1861–1952)/Fine
Art of Oakham Ltd., Leicestershire, UK; *Street Arabs at Play*, 1890 (oil on canvas),
Stanley, Dorothy, nee Tennant (1855–1926)/© Lady Lever Art Gallery, National
Museums Liverpool), 17 (*The Hornby Train*, 1951–53, Rogers, Claude Maurice
(1907–79)/Private Collection; *Family in the Park*, 1999 (oil on canvas), Bootman,
Colin (Contemporary Artist)/Private Collection) 68 (Sudden Shower at Atake,
from the series *One Hundred Views of Famous Places in Edo* (colour woodblock
print), Hiroshige, Ando or Utagawa (1797–1858)/Private Collection/Photo
© Christie's Images; *Clouds* (oil on canvas), Gotch, Thomas Cooper (1854–1931)
Private Collection/Photo © The Maas Gallery, London; *Bitter Cold* (oil on canvas),
Nichols, Dale William (1904–1995) Private Collection/Photo © Christie's
Images; *The Sun*, 1910–16 (mural), Munch, Edvard (1863–1944)/University of
Oslo, Norway/© DACS); Corbis p.50 (cat/Yann Arthus-Bertrand); Getty Images
pp.27 (Linda/Erin Patrice O'Brien/The Image Bank, Isabel/Tony Anderson/Taxi),
51 (sheep/Julia Thorne/Robert Harding World Imagery), 53 (Caleb/Insy Shah/
Gulfimages, Li/Sean Justice/Riser, Sally/LWA/The Image Bank, Meg/Ann
Cutting/Botanica, horse/Martin Ruegner/Photographer's Choice, duck/Mark
Harwood/Iconica), 60 (toddler/Martin Ruegner/Photographer's Choice, 4 year
old/Peter Cade/Stone), 61 (boy swimming/Laurence Monneret/Taxi, 7 year old/
Michael Malyszko/Taxi), 62 (eagle/Tom Murphy/National Geographic, read/
Bruce Laurance/The Image Bank, swim/David Madison/Stone, draw/John
Bradley/Stone, write/Anne Rippy/The Image Bank, juggle/Andreas Stirnberg/
Photographer's Choice), 76 (park/Bob Scott/Photonica), 78 (mother/Garry
Wade/Taxi, grandmother/Zia Soliel/Iconica, boy in hall/Vanessa Davies/Dorling
Kindersley, boy in garage/Tim Kitchen/The Image Bank); Oxford University
Press pp.18 (Ella), 27 (London, Rio, Cape Town, Istanbul), 52 (Ella, goats, chicks,
cows), 53 (cow), 62 (hop), 70, 78 (father, grandfather, girl in kitchen, girl in
garden); Photolibrary p.53 (huskie/Alexey Gnilenkov/Age footstock); Rex
Features p.77 (school/Andrew Price).